GETTING THE
MESSAGE

The Internet
and the World Wide Web

How to interpret
what we see, read and hear

Sean Connolly

FRANKLIN WATTS
LONDON • SYDNEY

 An Appleseed Editions book

First published in 2009 by Franklin Watts
338 Euston Road, London NW1 3BH

Franklin Watts Australia
Hachette Children's Books
Level 17/207 Kent St, Sydney, NSW 2000

© 2009 Appleseed Editions

Created by Appleseed Editions Ltd,
Well House, Friars Hill, Guestling,
East Sussex TN35 4ET

Designed by Helen James
Edited by Mary-Jane Wilkins
Picture research by Su Alexander

ISBN 978 0 7496 8782 3

Dewey Classification: 302.23

A CIP catalogue for this book is available from the British Library.

Photograph acknowledgements
page 7 David P Hall/Corbis; 8 Sergei Chirikov/EPA/Corbis; 10 ClassicStock/Alamy;
12 Masahiro Sano/Corbis; 15 Mozilla Firefox; 16 Jaubert Bernard/Alamy; 19 Joelle
Diderich/EPA/Corbis; 20 James Duncan Davidson; 22 Content Mine International/
Alamy; 24 Dennis Galante/Corbis; 26 Max Hammond/Alamy; 28 D Hurst/Alamy;
30 Plainpicture GMBH & Co.KG/Alamy; 32 Chris Rout/Alamy; 34 Ace Stock Limited/
Alamy; 37 Anne-Marie Palmer/Alamy; 38 ClassicStock/Alamy; 40 Ace Stock Limited/
Alamy; 42 Strauss/Curtis/Corbis
Front cover Strauss/Curtis/Corbis

Printed in China

Franklin Watts is a division of Hachette Children's Books,
an Hachette Livre UK company.
www.hachettelivre.co.uk

Contents

A new way of communicating   6

Weaving a Web   8

What's in a name?   12

The future is now   16

Web 2.0   20

You have a friend in me   24

Crash! Wipeout!   28

Identity theft   32

Threats to freedom?   34

The Web generation   38

The outlook for the Internet   42

Glossary   44

Further reading and website links   45

Index   46

A new way of communicating

As a rule, parents and teachers help young people to understand the media and how it works. They help them grasp how newspapers and magazines are published, how films and television programmes are produced and how advertisements are created and displayed.

Even if adults have never worked in these fields, they can speak from experience – after all, they have been reading and watching films and television all their lives. The Internet is different. It is young enough

– and changes fast enough – for the tables to be turned. Many adults claim to be slow to understand how it works, and children are as quick to claim the advantage of knowing as much about it as adults. Both groups are partly right – and partly wrong. And both could benefit from understanding it a bit more.

Getting to the core

First, people need to understand the difference between the Internet and the World Wide Web (see pages 12-15). Although many people use these terms interchangeably, they mean different things. Understanding basic differences such as this can make it easier for everyone to navigate through the world of Web pages, hypertext, e-mails and jpegs.

New dimensions

Like anything linked to fast-changing developments in technology, the Internet is exciting and constantly developing. Faster Internet connections mean that vast amounts of information – including moving images and sounds – can travel across the globe in an instant. This helps society in many ways, making it easier to study, keep in touch with friends, be entertained and to do business.

Recent advances have taken the Web into a new era of collaboration and feedback. Unlike media such as newspapers, magazines and even television, the Web invites users to become participants. People can respond to – and help shape – what they see or hear on the Web. This free exchange of ideas, sometimes called Web 2.0 (see pages 20-23), has created an entirely new way of exchanging information.

But with these changes come risks. Sharing information can put people at risk or spread falsehoods and unfounded accusations. Internet crime, including stealing people's banking details and even their identity, threatens to topple many of the freedoms that the Internet revolution has already provided – and promises for the future.

Opposite: high-speed Internet connections have brought the Web to many bedrooms, where young people can use their computers for entertainment, study or just to chat with friends.

7

Weaving a Web

It's hard to remember that as recently as 20 years ago hardly anyone used or even knew terms such as download, website or e-mail. The enormous change since then has been described as a revolution, a term which describes widespread developments that seem to affect every part of our world.

The Internet and its most widely used element, the World Wide Web, represent the cutting edge of these developments. Although they are constantly evolving, they already represent a combination of two other important elements – communications technology and computers.

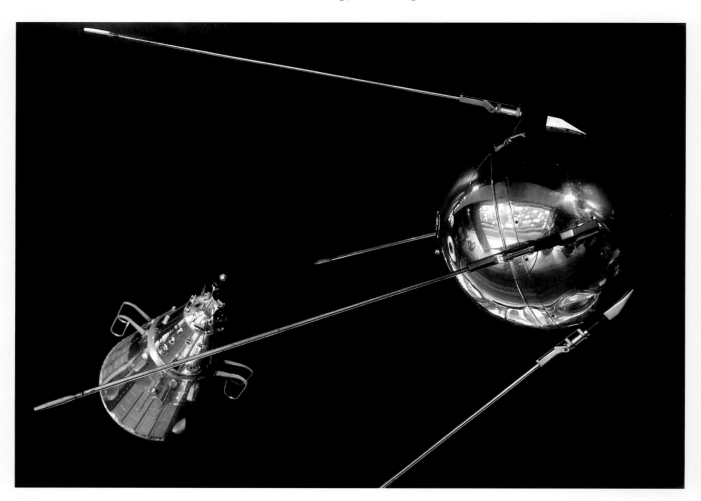

Parallel developments

At the most basic level, the Internet can be described as a huge network of computers linked together through telephone technology. The first computers and telephones were developed during the nineteenth century, but it was during the twentieth century that both really progressed.

Computers began as relatively simple calculating machines, able to do sums and work with basic mathematics. Through the twentieth century, however, computer experts found many new purposes for their machines, which also became more powerful – and eventually smaller.

Telephones changed from being playthings of the rich in a few cities to being vital elements in a world communications network. It was only a matter of time before someone found a way to link the growing power of computers to the instant communication provided by telephones.

From the army to the household

By the mid-1950s, the United States and the Soviet Union were enemies in the Cold War as well as rivals over technology. The Soviets beat the Americans into space by launching the first orbiting satellite, Sputnik, in 1957. The United States wanted to regain the advantage, and began to develop a system to link computers in different universities and other research centres across the country.

The government body in charge of developing this system of linked computers was called the Advanced Research Projects Agency (ARPA). By 1969 ARPA had developed its first network of four university computers. The network became known as ARPANET and in the 1970s it was expanded to include computers in the UK and other countries.

The word Internet first appeared in 1974, and originally described a system of sending information on the ARPANET. The development of the first personal computers (PCs) in the following year was the real breakthrough: until then only universities, government departments

Opposite: Sputnik (right) is basic compared with the hundreds of satellites that have come after it. But the significance of this small metal ball is huge: high-speed communications such as the Internet depend on satellites to relay information in an instant.

and other large organizations could be linked on the ARPANET system. By 1975, Bill Gates and other software developers could see that linking PCs around the world would be the way forward, so they began working to achieve that goal.

Birth of the Web

By the late 1980s, the term Internet had become common to describe the network that had begun as ARPANET. But it was still quite limited, mainly just sending and receiving e-mails. The British scientist Tim Berners-Lee took the Internet into its next major phase by developing the World Wide Web in 1989, and in the following year the original ARPANET ended.

The World Wide Web (often called simply the Web) uses the Internet to send and receive complex information. It does this by using hypertext to link the millions of documents that are available. This allows users to view or receive pictures or movies, hear sound files or simply read text. All these developments – unimaginable even when ARPANET was developed – are now available on even the smallest of computers.

Computers in the 1960s were huge and confusing to anyone but an expert. Yet the first steps along the information superhighway were made by using these slow, bulky machines.

SPOTLIGHT ON
The first e-mail

In 1971, computer expert Ray Tomlinson was working for a company called Bolt Beranek and Newman, based in Cambridge, Massachusetts. That company had been chosen by the US Department of Defense to develop the ARPANET, a network of computers that was a forerunner of the Internet.

Tomlinson and others at his company had already found ways of writing messages for other computer users. But these messages had to be read on the same computer as they were written and sent. Tomlinson found a way of combining this message-writing system with the ARPANET system – making it possible to send messages from one computer to another. The first e-mail was sent from one computer to another just next to it. But although the two computers were in the same room, they were only connected through the ARPANET network. And the first e-mail said? According to Tomlinson, it was not a dramatic message, just 'something like QWERTYUIOP', referring to the top line of letters on a keyboard.

Tomlinson's first meaningful e-mail came soon afterwards. In that message, he announced the arrival of network e-mail and he introduced the e-mail address system, including the @ sign to mean 'at'. A new chapter in communications had begun.

TALKING HEADS

EARLY E-MAILS

Ray Tomlinson, who developed the idea of e-mail communications, was recently asked how the early use of e-mail differed from the way we use it today. 'The early uses were not terribly different from the current uses. The exceptions were that there was only plain text in the messages and there was no spam.'

What's in a name?

During the 1980s and early 1990s, the Internet was often described as being part of the information superhighway. The American term superhighway describes multi-lane motorways on which vehicles can travel quickly over long distances. In those days, people knew that new technologies such as fibre-optic cables, mobile phones and satellite television were replacing the communications technology of the time.

For these people, the Internet was another lane of this superhighway because they saw it as being similar to the other technologies. Like the others it seemed to be linked to existing technologies – computers and telephones, in the

Fibre-optic phone lines, which channel information along beams of light, have helped the Internet operate far faster and with fewer interruptions.

case of the Internet. But soon it became clear that the Internet offered far more than people originally imagined. And in a curious reversal of terms, the Internet can be said to have become the information superhighway and not simply remained an element of it.

A widening range

It is easy to be overwhelmed by the complexity of the Internet and by the constantly growing and changing elements that form it. Part of the confusion comes from the names people use, both officially and informally. Understanding some of the basic differences in these terms helps to give a clear overall picture of how it all works.

The Internet (or Net), strictly speaking, describes linked computers. Like the original ARPANET computers (see page 9), the computers depend on some form of telephone connection. That connection can take the form of traditional copper wires and more modern fibre-optic cables. Just like ordinary telephone networks, it can also use wireless technology to send signals through the connection.

If we go back to the first images people used for new technology in the 1980s, it becomes clear that the Internet really has become the information superhighway. In other words, this growing network of linked computers is the route that other elements take to travel from computer to computer.

That image is important in order to understand something that computer people try to explain to everyone else: the Internet and the World Wide Web (or Web) are not just two ways of describing the same thing. The Web is an enormous collection of linked resources. The Web could not operate – sending resources such as documents, images and sound clips from computer to computer – without the Internet as its 'highway'. So the Internet and Web are as separate (but in some ways, also linked) as rail lines are for trains.

SPOTLIGHT ON
Clients, servers and browser wars

Millions of people rely on the information the Web provides. But few understand how it is sent and received. When there are so many files on the Web, how are they found, sent and received so quickly? At the heart of the Web are client–server relationships. Every computer user looking for information is a client. Someone reading a Web page on the UK Labour party might click on a hypertext link on Tony Blair to learn more about the former prime minister. That click would trigger the computer's Web browser to contact the website that had the UK Labour party Web page, requesting the page with information on Tony Blair.

The website in this example is the server. It has the information – in the form of Web pages – to give the clients who might ask for it. And just as clients (individual computer users) need Web browsers to make their way around the Web, computers containing websites need special software to supply their information to clients. That software is called a Web server program. As the Web grows and produces enormous amounts of business, there is fierce competition to provide Web servers and

browsers. The companies which produce software to do this can make a great deal of money. Most computers are clients rather than servers, so the competition to dominate the world of Web browsers is strong.

The experience of software giant Microsoft shows how even a powerful company needs to be constantly alert in the fast-changing world of the Internet and the Web. Despite being the world's most successful software company by the 1980s, Microsoft was slow to realize how important the Web would become. By the late 1990s, a rival company (Netscape) had become the leading Web browser. Microsoft then introduced Internet Explorer (IE), which it provided free (unlike Netscape). It also added Internet Explorer to the Windows software packages that came with new computers.

Soon, IE had gained most of the Web browser market. But it failed to improve on Netscape, allowing other browsers to come in with better products. Mozilla Firefox did just that in 2004, offering a simpler way of moving around the Web. By mid-2008 Firefox had almost one-fifth of the browser market.

Mozilla Firefox is a Web browser that has captured nearly 20 per cent of the market. Firefox is one of the leading examples of open-source software – software that is made available free and which users can improve or change without being penalized. This aim ties in with the democratic ideals of Tim Berners-Lee, who developed the Web.

The future is now

People are spending more and more time online, as the Internet has crept further into their lives. The main advantages of the Net – speed and convenience – have helped new companies thrive and have given older companies the chance to broaden the way in which they do business.

One breakthrough in the business use of the Web came when companies found ways for people to pay for goods and services online. By entering details of their credit card or bank account, people can pay bills, book holidays, buy birthday presents or download music and films. People still have concerns about the safety of these online transactions, and some have found that their most private financial information has been picked up by dishonest Web users (see page 27).

On the whole, however, the Web has made it possible to turn what once seemed a dream – being able to deal with the world from the comfort of a bedroom or an office – into a

Tiny MP3 players such as iPods are typical of the constant move towards smaller, more powerful technology. Many portable devices such as phones have Internet access.

SPOTLIGHT ON
The recording industry

Popular music became a major industry in the 1950s and continues to generate billions of pounds' worth of sales each year. But although people might still be prepared to buy recordings of some of the artists of the 1950s – such as Elvis Presley, Chuck Berry and Frank Sinatra – very few people would buy the same type of recording now.

Recordings in the 1950s were sold as vinyl records, either as singles (one song on each side of the record) or as albums (with four or five songs per side). Record players needed to be level, free from dust and protected from bumps and vibrations – otherwise the records would not play and might be damaged. In an attempt to solve these problems, from the 1970s the music industry began to produce albums in other forms, such as cassettes and eight-track cartridges. Eventually CDs (compact discs) overtook all other forms of recording in the 1990s, promising perfect sound coupled with durability.

At the same time, new software allowed computers to download and play sound files with audio quality which matched that of CDs. The twenty-first century has seen the next phase in selling – and listening to – music. Sales of CDs are falling by more than ten per cent a year worldwide as people are choosing to download music and transfer it to portable MP3 players. More than 170 million of the most popular type of MP3 player, the Apple iPod, have been sold since they were launched in 2001. The Apple website that provides the music for downloads, iTunes, has sold more than five billion songs in that same period.

Musicians and record labels now offer their music on websites which allow listeners to download (for a fee) individual songs or albums. This commercial set-up has changed since the year 2000. At that time, a number of websites offered the chance to download music free of charge. Musicians and recording companies argued that such free swaps of music broke copyright laws, which protect the rights of artists and writers and ensure that they are paid for their work. Much of the free music sharing ended when the most famous free download company, Napster, was driven out of business because they became involved in expensive court cases involving copyright law.

reality. The future – even as it was imagined as recently as the 1980s – really is now.

These advances show how the Web both reflects and directs some of the changes in the way people live. Instant banking or shopping saves people time and effort. But if these become the only ways to do business, then some people might find that they miss the chance to bump into other people in the real world.

Opposite: Radiohead lead singer and songwriter Thom Yorke has supported freer access to his band's music (via downloads) for several years.

FOR WHAT IT'S WORTH

RADIOHEAD OFFERED THEIR FANS A CHANCE TO CHOOSE HOW MUCH (IF ANYTHING) THEY WERE WILLING TO PAY FOR THEIR ALBUM IN RAINBOWS, WHICH THEY MADE AVAILABLE AS A DOWNLOAD IN OCTOBER 2007. THE MUSIC INDUSTRY – AND OTHER BANDS – WATCHED TO SEE HOW MUCH PEOPLE WOULD CHOOSE TO PAY.

THE FIGURES FOR THE FIRST MONTH OF ALBUM SALES WERE INTERESTING. NEARLY TWO-THIRDS (62 PER CENT) OF PEOPLE WORLDWIDE CHOSE TO PAY ABSOLUTELY NOTHING FOR THE ALBUM, AND THE AVERAGE PRICE PAID BY THE OTHER 38 PER CENT WAS ABOUT £2.90. THAT IS CONSIDERABLY LESS THAN THE COST OF SIMILAR ALBUMS AT THE APPLE ITUNES STORE AND SIMILAR WEB OUTLETS.

HOW MUCH WOULD YOU BE PREPARED TO PAY FOR AN ALBUM BY ONE OF YOUR FAVOURITE ARTISTS? WHAT ARE THE ARGUMENTS FOR – AND AGAINST – OFFERING CUSTOMERS SUCH A CHOICE? WOULD A PAY-AS-YOU-PLEASE SYSTEM HELP OR HURT ARTISTS WHO ARE BEGINNING THEIR CAREERS?

Over to YOU

TALKING HEADS

AUCTION GIANT

'Ever seen an old western – where all of a sudden the cavalry rides in? That's what we do.' Randy Wigginton is referring to his role on the eBay SWAT team, a group of software specialists who need to solve problems as soon as they crop up. Wigginton's experience as one of Apple's chief programmers – leading to his problem-solving skills – has helped eBay grow into the largest online auction website. In 2008, eBay was the third website in popularity, according to how many minutes UK Internet users spent on it. Only MSN Messenger and Facebook scored higher, and eBay accounted for 1.7 billion online minutes from UK Internet users.

Web 2.0

Every industry has its own ways of describing products. Car-makers release new models every year, hoping that drivers will be eager to buy this year's model and will trade in their old one. People working with computers – or more specifically, with computer software – use a numbering system to show which software version is loaded on to a computer. The first version of a product is usually 1.0; the second is 2.0, moving on to 3.0, 4.0 and so on.

Bearded and informal, Tim O'Reilly is like so many leaders in Web technology. He argues that Web 2.0 is a chance for the Web to break down barriers and become even more democratic.

Internet experts come from this computer software background, so it is not surprising that they call the new generation of Web applications Web 2.0. Version 2.0 of some software packages involves only a slight tinkering with a successful product – a bit like slight changes to a new car model. Is Web 2.0 another slight tinkering with a familiar system? Or is it – as many experts describe it – a revolution in the way we use the Internet, and run our lives?

New attitudes

The Internet has come to represent speed and instant communication – especially when users have a fast broadband connection. Vast amounts of information can be viewed or sent from one computer to another. But there is another aspect of the Internet that taps into a free-spirited sense of democracy and freedom. Because the Web represents a new way of doing so many things, many want as little outside control as possible – either from governments or big, established companies. For them, the Web is a way to share information and ideas rather than a money-making opportunity.

Tim Berners-Lee, the developer of the Web, is an example of someone who holds this idealistic view. During the 1980s, as more and more people bought personal computers, software companies earned large amounts of money by charging royalties for their ideas. Berners-Lee, on the other hand,

TALKING HEADS

NEW RULES FOR SUCCESS

'Web 2.0 is the business revolution in the computer industry caused by the move to the Internet as platform, and an attempt to understand the rules for success on that new platform.'

Tim O'Reilly, the software expert believed to be the originator of the term Web 2.0.

SPOTLIGHT ON
The Wikipedia debate

People often spend hundreds of pounds buying encyclopedias that promise in-depth information about thousands of subjects. But these expensive sets of books soon become out of date.

One solution, in the Web 2.0 era, has come in the form of online enyclopedias that can be constantly amended – either by readers or by those who write each entry. Wikipedia is the best-known online encyclopedia. It has a carefully constructed system allowing articles to be written, approved, called into question, updated or rejected – all by readers.

This system sounds wonderful, and many people believe it is. But others note that people can easily rewrite articles about themselves – or people's enemies can add wounding material to articles about them. It is also much harder to prove the accuracy of newly added information. Another criticism centres on the relative importance of different articles – and whether it is a good idea to decide on their length in this democratic way. The article on former British prime minister John Major, for example, is only a little longer than the Homer Simpson entry.

No one doubts that Homer, Bart and Marge are part of a clever, funny television programme, but are Wikipedia's priorities right if its entry on The Simpsons is longer than its entry on Asia?

believed that the world would benefit much more if such information became freely available. He therefore received no fee for developing the World Wide Web in 1990 or for creating the first website in 1991. And in 1994, he helped persuade companies working with the Web to use royalty-free technology. The Web has blossomed because of the freedom to create and distribute information.

Being active and interactive

One major aspect of the Web 2.0 era centres on how interactive people's Web activity has become. Initially, the Web offered a very fast way to send information to people's computers. This flow of information was largely one-way: from the information provider to the user in the same way information travels to a radio or TV set. The interactive approach allows users to send information back, and even to update and change the nature of the information at its source.

Thousands of websites rely on this interactive approach. For example, people can read the experiences and opinions of other travellers or diners about tourist attractions, hotels and restaurants. They, in turn, can add their opinions so that others will have a fuller picture. In the same way, readers of newspapers can check their online versions to respond immediately to articles and to carry on political debates – in real time – with other readers.

KNOWLEDGE OR DRIVEL?

DO YOU THINK THAT WEB 2.0 ENCYCLOPEDIAS SUCH AS WIKIPEDIA ENCOURAGE A BETTER – AND MORE IMMEDIATE – SPREAD OF INFORMATION? OR DO YOU THINK THAT AN ENCYCLOPEDIA SHOULD HAVE A PERSON OR EDITORIAL TEAM WHO DECIDES HOW MUCH SPACE EACH ARTICLE DESERVES – AND THAT THE WIKIPEDIA APPROACH ENCOURAGES NONSENSE POSING AS KNOWLEDGE?

You have a friend in me

The interactive nature of the Web 2.0 era has taken computer users in new directions. Although the Web is where many of these advances are happening, the tide of change has swept across the whole Internet.

Many people forget that the Internet was interactive – allowing back and forth communication – well before the Web was developed. Usenet (the words 'user' and 'network' combined) was developed in 1979. It was first seen as a poor man's ARPANET (see pages 9-11), but this Internet

Spotlight on
Netiquette

Children often complain about having to learn the rules of behaviour that we call etiquette. But at their heart, these rules are simply a way of teaching good manners, which can be described as behaving in a way that puts other people at ease. There is nothing stuffy or old-fashioned about listening to the other side in an argument, not swearing at strangers or being kind.

These principles are just as important in the virtual world of Usenet groups, social networking sites or in any of the ways in which people communicate with each other on the Internet. The Internet Guide, a website that sheds light on a range of Internet subjects, offers sensible pointers on Internet etiquette, or netiquette. They include:

• Not using someone else's name and pretending to be that person.
• Not using abusive or threatening language.
• Not posting remarks about people's sexuality, race or gender.
• Not trying to obtain or use someone else's password.
• Not trying to obtain personal information about someone.

Some of these might seem obvious, but people sometimes lose track of the fact that they are dealing with other people when they are online.

Opposite: these friends might record their fun by uploading photos on to a social network site. No one loses through that sort of innocent fun, but university students and employees may regret posting embarrassing photos of themselves.

discussion system still thrives. Users read and post public messages, usually following on from each other in the way a conversation flows. Strings (or threads) of messages can cover all sorts of topics, from favourite television programmes to politics and health issues.

Even older than Usenet is e-mail, which began in the 1960s and was a building block of the Internet itself. So it is clear that one of the main attractions of advances in computers was the opportunity to send information back and forth from one computer to another.

And that ability to communicate has continued to drive new Internet thinking – whether it leads to smaller devices, wireless connections or combinations with mobile phones.

An obvious step

It is hardly surprising, then, that people looked for ways to combine the communications heart of the Internet with all the advances the Web has brought to the world. YouTube and other video-sharing websites offer users a chance to post and view videos. Although it was only founded in 2005, YouTube has already proved to be enormously popular and influential. It has played an important role in making international stars out of unknown musicians and in influencing national elections.

The Internet has drawn millions of people into virtual communities, but in real life many of them spend hours on their own.

One of the most dramatic advances in the Internet has come through social networking sites. Sites such as Facebook, MySpace, Bebo and MSN Spaces have attracted millions of members. Each of these sites

gives users a chance to set up their own page, where they can tell the rest of the Internet world about themselves – their background, favourite activities and their plans in life. Social networking sites have been described as being the village greens of the twenty-first century – places where people can meet friends and make new ones.

Users can personalize their pages with music, videos and blogs; a messaging service allows members of the same network to become 'friends' and to exchange information. Most of these sites have a minimum age and they offer guidance on how to avoid some of the risks that users can face (see page 39).

Those risks are often the side-effect of the features that make these websites so attractive. People often upload quizzes, games and intelligence tests on to their personal pages, encouraging their online friends to do the same. These extras are known as applications. To work properly, applications need to use some of the user's personal details. Usually that is not a problem, but if a dishonest person creates such an application, then he or she can find out a great deal about the website users – without their realizing it.

So, while people enjoy the chance to make new friends and widen their social horizons, they also run the risk of encountering some uninvited guests.

Over to YOU

OUT OF TOUCH WITH THE REAL WORLD?
IN JULY 2008, LONDON-BASED PSYCHIATRIST DR HIMANSHU TYAGI EXPRESSED SOME OF HIS FEARS ABOUT THE SPREAD OF SOCIAL NETWORKING SITES: 'IT MAY BE POSSIBLE THAT YOUNG PEOPLE WHO HAVE NO EXPERIENCE OF A WORLD WITHOUT ONLINE SOCIETIES PUT LESS VALUE ON THEIR REAL WORLD IDENTITIES.' DO YOU AGREE WITH HIS CONCLUSION?

Crash! Wipeout!

The Web has opened up all sorts of ways of doing business, studying and communicating with other people in an instant (see pages 20-23). This has been of great benefit to many people – especially those living in remote areas or those who must stay at home because of illness or injury. As more people are using faster Internet connections, the benefits look set to grow quickly in the future.

It is hard – if not impossible – to understand why software experts create viruses that can shut down a computer, or even thousands of computers. Computer users need to constantly update their anti-virus software to protect themselves from this danger.

The key word in the previous paragraph is 'quickly', because it is the speed of the Internet (as well as the speed of its growth) that has led to sudden setbacks for some people. It is not surprising that a means of communication built on speed attracted people who were involved with 'get rich quick' schemes.

The Internet has a free atmosphere and is less controlled by government watchdogs than the television, radio and telephone industries. So it attracts people who are prepared to take advantage of the innocent (see Spotlight on Web scams, page 31).

The industries surrounding the Internet have also tempted people to take big gambles with their savings. When people lost money after putting it into Web-based companies, some observers suggested that the Internet boom was over. Others argued that the world was only just beginning to understand how this new industry operated, and that soon people would be able to distinguish the good opportunities from the more risky ones. Either way, people are still learning some hard lessons about how the Internet and the world of business relate to each other.

Dot-com boom – and bust

Like some parts of the computing industry, the Internet and the Web have developed very quickly. Vast numbers of online companies developed in the late 1990s (see page 30). Businesses associated with the Web – known as dot-com companies because of their Web addresses – seemed to guarantee success as they represented the future of the business world.

Dot-com companies tended not to follow the usual advice for new businesses, which is to grow at a steady rate, make a profit and then use some of that profit to build the business a little more. Instead they used the enormous amount of money that people invested in them to grow before they ever made any money. The idea was to grow and grow, becoming widely known for a service that began by being cheap or even free, and then eventually to start charging people for services that would make a profit.

Things did not happen quite as the dot-com businesses – and the people who invested money in them – expected. At first, everything seemed fine: the value of dot-com shares continued to rise, although many of the most famous dot-com companies were losing money.

Eventually, the dot-com bubble burst. With so much of their value tied up in what investors felt the companies could be worth – rather than in traditional value such as profit and a proven track record – the dot-com companies ran the risk of losing value if investors lost confidence.

That is exactly what happened in March 2000. People started selling their shares in dot-com companies, driving down their value rapidly. Many dot-com companies went out of business shortly afterwards. Others cut back considerably and operated with more traditional methods. The Internet and the Web might have entered the business world – but centuries of business practice had the final say.

Elderly people living on their own can often be tricked by dishonest e-mails promising services or products for 'just a small fee'. Too often they reveal important banking details.

SPOTLIGHT ON

Web scams

One of the biggest risks that Internet users face is losing their money because of a scam. Dishonest people are constantly finding ways of persuading innocent people to send them money – or even to disclose their personal banking details. The scam could be in the form of a plea to give to a charity (which turns out not to exist), an ad for a quick and easy loan (the borrower just needs to send £100 to set it up), or a fake announcement that the reader has just won a lottery jackpot (which cannot pay out until a small sum of money is sent).

The approaches change all the time, and many of them seem genuine at first. It is the first mistake that leads people into further trouble. A recent e-mail in the UK was a good example. It claimed to be from the government department that collects taxes and told readers that they had paid too much tax and were due to have some refunded.

The snag was that taxpayers needed either to respond to the e-mail or to go to a website where they were asked for bank or credit card details. Why? Because the government was eager to pay people quickly, and that meant directly into their accounts. Except, once the unsuspecting people passed on these details, they found that they received no money and that someone – somewhere – had the information to take money from their accounts.

TALKING HEADS

TALKING HEAD

'Despite all the warning signs, it never occurred to me that I was working in a bubble. Until it popped. I don't want to make that mistake again. The three years after the bubble burst were dark, dark times for software developers. Everyone had to scramble to find a place to weather the worst of the storm. And the backlash was severe: rampant offshoring, devaluation of the IT industry as a whole, and diminished salaries and opportunities for everyone.' Software expert Jeff Atwood writing in his blog *Coding Horror*.

Identity theft

At the beginning of the thriller *The Day of the Jackal,* a hired murderer finds the grave of someone who was born the year he was, but who died as a child. The murderer then finds the dead boy's birth certificate and uses it as his own when he applies for a UK passport. He receives a passport in the other person's name and travels with it as he plans his crimes.

People can protect themselves from identity theft by shredding important documents such as bank statements. It can be harder to destroy Internet banking details.

It was never quite as easy to steal someone else's identity as author Frederick Forsyth described in his novel, but the idea certainly appealed to criminals. The age of computer records and the Internet now make it easier – and much quicker – for criminals to find someone else's records and use them for their own activities.

The victims of these crimes are not long-dead people, as in the book, but ordinary people. Only when they check their bank statements or other financial records do they discover that someone – somehow – has been taking money from their account. With all the information that is available because governments now promise to be more open, dishonest people are finding new ways to steal money from the innocent or careless.

Complicated business

Identity theft is a type of fraud, a crime that is notoriously difficult to prove in a court of law. Because investigations are so difficult and costly, the police can only pursue about one per cent of such activities, according to CIFAS, the UK Fraud Prevention Service. Organized crime operates successfully in this shady area partly because it is so complicated. Today, Internet and mobile phone users should follow the CIFAS advice about protecting their identity, to avoid being conned by a clever criminal.

SPOTLIGHT ON ID theft cases

CIFAS records every case of identity theft reported in the UK. In less than a decade, the number of reports have risen by more than 800 per cent:

Year	Identity theft cases recorded
1999	9,000
2000	16,000
2001	24,000
2002	34,000
2003	46,000
2004	56,000
2005	66,000
2006	80,000
2007	77,500

The slight drop from 2006 to 2007 probably represents increased awareness of identity theft, so people are now taking precautions which make it harder to tap into their money information.

Threats to freedom?

Nearly everyone who uses the Internet agrees that it offers a new view of freedom. The quantity of information available seems endless, and users can turn many of their dreams into reality – or at least virtual reality. With just a few clicks of the mouse, people can go rafting down rapids in New Zealand, listen to lions at an African watering hole, or take a stroll down Fifth Avenue in the heart of New York City.

But many people believe this freedom comes at a cost, and that the cost could be wider freedoms – the right to enjoy a life free from snooping and the right to be confident that some information is not available to the outside world. In addition to the viruses and advertisements that arrive uninvited (see page 28), Internet

Websites can help students understand some complex writing, such as Shakespeare's plays. But young people should make sure that they use the Web as a tool – and not use it to do their work for them (for example, by buying coursework essays).

Spotlight on
Web cheating

During their years at university, students reading many subjects need to write long essays. These essays help university teachers judge how well the students understand their subject; some of them count towards their final degree. People with top degrees have a better chance of finding a good job after university.

Because of these high stakes, some students are tempted to buy essays online and submit them to their teachers as though they had written the essays themselves. Many websites offering these essays claim that they are not meant to take the place of people's own work – rather, they are intended to help students learn more about a subject. Whether or not this is true, a number of students download paid-for essays and pass them off as their own work.

This sort of cheating is known as plagiarism and it is a serious offence at university. Many cheats do not realize that teachers can usually identify an essay which seems odd and unlike anything the student has written before. Also, universities can turn the tables on cheats by submitting their essays to another website, which analyses them phrase by phrase to see whether it has been taken from elsewhere. The punishment for students found to have cheated in this way is expulsion from university – an extreme price to pay for their laziness.

users can find themselves host to other unwanted visitors. By using cookies, companies and other organizations can track people's habits as they browse the Web. Worse still, especially for young people who might upload wild party photos to share with online friends (see pages 24-25), universities and employers can check social networking sites to see how people behave in their own time. At times it can seem as though people have lost any sense of privacy when it comes to the Internet.

All these issues go right to the heart of the Internet and threaten some of the ease and freedom that people have come to associate with it. The idealists who developed the Web and those who continue to promote free software typify the best of the Internet – a willingness to spread and share knowledge without looking for personal gain. Some of the changes taking place – such as increased advertising and government snooping – could transform the Web permanently.

Opposite: modern societies face difficult decisions about protecting the wider population – and the individuals who are part of it. Is computer snooping by the police acceptable if it prevents criminals carrying out dangerous acts?

TALKING HEADS

DON'T BLAME THE MESSENGER

Tim Berners-Lee, developer of the World Wide Web, is widely admired for his refusal to become an Internet billionaire because of his work. America's *Time* magazine summed up his efforts neatly when it listed him as one of the 100 most influential people of the twentieth century: 'He designed it. He loosed it on the world. And he more than anyone else has fought to keep it open, non-proprietary and free.'

While understandably proud of his achievement – and the countless developments that have sprung from it – Berners-Lee recognizes that the Web can also be used to limit people's freedom. Dishonest people, or simply those with an interest in quick profits, can find ways of tracking how others use the Web, gathering detailed information about their buying habits, holiday preferences and even romantic ideals.

Despite this negative side, Berners-Lee remains sure that the Web should not be governed or restricted too heavily by any organization. He continues to be committed to developing technology that 'supports a just and fair planet but remember, it's not the technology's role to make the rules or enforce them... We can't blame the technology when we make mistakes.'

TOO MUCH POWER?

THE UK GOVERNMENT HAS INTRODUCED LAWS THAT ALLOW COUNCILS (LOCAL GOVERNMENTS) TO SNOOP ON PEOPLE AS PART OF THE BATTLE AGAINST TERRORISM. SINCE 2000, THE REGULATION OF INVESTIGATORY POWERS (RIP) ACT HAS ALLOWED COUNCILS TO LOOK THROUGH PEOPLE'S TELEPHONE, INTERNET AND E-MAIL RECORDS.

MORE RECENTLY, THE ACT HAS COME UNDER FIRE. ONE ARGUMENT AGAINST IT IS BASED ON THE PRINCIPLES OF CIVIL RIGHTS. MANY PEOPLE BELIEVE THAT THE ACT GIVES TOO MUCH POWER TO LOCAL GOVERNMENTS, AND THAT BRITISH PEOPLE MAY LOSE MANY OF THEIR INDIVIDUAL FREEDOMS. ON ANOTHER LEVEL, CRITICS ARGUE THAT SOME COUNCILS ARE WRONGLY USING THE ACT AS AN EXCUSE TO TRACK DOWN PEOPLE WHOSE DOGS HAVE FOULED THE PAVEMENTS OR WHO HAVE LEFT LITTER IN PUBLIC PLACES.

DO YOU THINK THAT ANY GOVERNMENTS – NATIONAL OR LOCAL – SHOULD HAVE THE POWER TO INVESTIGATE PEOPLE IN THIS WAY? DOES THE THREAT OF TERRORISM AFFECT THIS ARGUMENT AT ALL?

Over to YOU

The Web generation

Every new generation of young people has to adjust to things their parents didn't know about when they were young. Less than a hundred years ago, young people in Europe and North America whose parents had not seen cars when they were young would soon learn to drive. Later generations found that they were the ones teaching about new technologies – first radio, then television and eventually computers.

That trend has continued into the age of the Internet. Young people are using the Net more and more, taking advantage of the new freedom but also exposing themselves to new risks. Once again, some parents and other adults feel that they are fighting a losing battle to keep up with a fast-changing world.

Both sides can learn from the other. Parents will benefit from being able to use the Net more confidently. Any young person who has seen a parent get to

Some people believe that life goes round in circles. Some of the parents who complain today about their children's Web activities spent much of their youth absorbed in their own activities.

Spotlight on
Staying safe on the Internet

Generations of young people have absorbed advice and warnings from their parents about avoiding people who might want to hurt or molest them. Unfortunately, it is easier for young people to be tricked by such dangerous people if they encounter them through the Net.

Children as young as nine or ten often visit websites where people exchange information about themselves. They believe what they read on these pages: that other people writing about themselves are also about the same age and interested in sharing ideas about their favourite music, films or hobbies. Unfortunately, some adults take advantage of children through these websites. These people may pose as children, as there is little or no way of proving how old others on the site are. Young people need to be aware of these dangers when using the Internet, and learn how to stay safe. ConnectSafely, a site promoting Internet safety, offers some basic guidelines for young people, especially when they are using social networking websites:

• Be your own person: don't let friends persuade you to pretend to be someone you are not.
• Be nice online: some aggressive Internet behaviour is a type of revenge.
• Think about what you post: even friends can use material against you.
• Read between the lines: be careful if people seem over-friendly towards you – they might have another motive.
• Don't talk about sex with strangers: this might seem obvious, but many young people ignore this advice.
• Avoid face to face meetings: the only way that someone can physically harm you is by being in the same place.
• Use these websites:
http://safekids.com/
http://internet-security.suite101.com/article.cfm/internet_sexual_predators

grips with e-mails or Web purchases for the first time will agree with that. But young, experienced Internet users should not lose sight of the fact that many of the risks they face – even though they seem tied to the new technology – are simply variations of age-old tricks and dangers. Their parents might be able to advise them on using the Net carefully, even if they aren't quite sure how to do just that themselves.

Worrying figures

Americans have been studying the online risks faced by children for years. Two leading groups, the Crimes against Children Research Center and the Kaiser Family Foundation, have found that certain groups are even more at risk than others. According to their findings:

• One in five American teenagers has had an unwanted sexual advance via the Web;

• Only one in four of those children told a parent about the online advance;

• 75 per cent of children are willing to share personal information about themselves and their family in exchange for goods and services;

• More than one-fifth of the targeted children were aged between ten and 13.

Today's Web generation will become the decision-making adults of tomorrow. Will they look back at the time they spent online and decide it was important or will they steer their own children away from the computer screen?

HAVING A GO AT TEACHERS

A YEAR 8 GIRL AT A SCHOOL IN SOUTHERN ENGLAND ORGANIZED A FUND-RAISING MUSIC EVENING IN HER TOWN, AND THE MONEY BEING RAISED WENT TO A LOCAL CHARITY. THE EVENT WAS A GREAT SUCCESS, WITH TEACHERS AND STUDENTS PERFORMING TO A PACKED HALL. SEVERAL PEOPLE, INCLUDING THE GIRL WHO ORGANIZED THE EVENING, FILMED PARTS OF THE EVENING AND UPLOADED THE FILM TO A VIDEO-SHARING WEBSITE.

SOME OF THESE VIDEOS, INCLUDING THOSE UPLOADED BY THE ORGANIZER, POKED FUN AT THE PEOPLE WHO TOOK PART. IN HER COMMENTARY, THE GIRL REFERRED TO SOME OF THE TEACHERS USING INSULTING TERMS THAT WOULD NOT BE ALLOWED IN SCHOOL. WHEN THE SCHOOL LEARNED ABOUT THESE INSULTING VIDEOS, THE GIRL WAS TOLD TO TAKE THEM DOWN FROM THE SITE. SHE WAS ALSO DISCIPLINED IN FRONT OF A SCHOOL ASSEMBLY AND WARNED THAT ONE MORE OFFENCE, NO MATTER HOW SMALL, WOULD LEAD TO HER EXPULSION FROM SCHOOL.

NO ONE DENIED THAT THE GIRL WAS WRONG TO UPLOAD VIDEOS WITH INSULTING COMMENTS, BUT WAS THE SCHOOL RIGHT TO DISCIPLINE HER FOR SOMETHING THAT HAPPENED AWAY FROM SCHOOL AND OUT OF SCHOOL HOURS? DO YOU THINK THE FACT THAT IT WAS A CHARITY EVENT SHOULD HAVE LESSENED HER PUNISHMENT?

Over to YOU

The outlook for the Internet

Predicting the future is tricky because it is so easy to base our predictions on ideas or theories that turn out to be wrong, or because we are unaware of some important change which might be lurking just around the corner.

A young South African uses a laptop to access the Web. The real Internet revolution will come when people in poorer countries begin to benefit from the advantages of the Web and other aspects of the Internet.

Two examples make it easier to understand this. During the 1960s experts were asked to look 20 years into the future and describe life as they imagined it would be then. Many of them believed that the world would rely on plastic in nearly every area of life by the 1980s. What they did not foresee was how much the price of oil (the basic raw material for producing plastic) would rise. On the other hand,

very few people in the late 1980s (just before the development of the World Wide Web) could have imagined how the Internet would dominate people's lives in the early twenty-first century.

Replacing the crystal ball

If we imagine the future today, we can safely assume that the Internet and the Web will continue to play an important role in people's lives. That role is likely to increase as more and more parts of the world become connected for the first time. And as more people, in different parts of the world, are hooked up, then everyone will benefit. The freer exchange of knowledge will help to raise living standards, improve health and medical treatment and allow people in poorer countries to develop new ways of earning income.

That is just part of the story for those who see the Internet continuing to do things better, more cheaply and faster. These optimists point to high-tech advances in technology that have boosted Internet connections for wireless hand-held devices, on the one hand, and low-cost developments, such as the $100 laptop project, that are opening up the Net to more and more people, on the other hand.

Opposing voices suggest that tough times lie ahead. Some people believe that the days of a free and easy Internet are numbered, with governments and private companies planning to limit privacy and to find new ways of charging for what is now free on the Net. It could be that both sides are right, but experts know enough to expect the unexpected – and to try to plan for it.

Over to YOU

YOUR CALL

WHERE DO YOU STAND ON THE ISSUE OF THE FUTURE OF THE INTERNET? DO YOU SEE IT MOVING FROM STRENGTH TO STRENGTH, CONTINUING TO OFFER UNEXPECTED BENEFITS FOR ALL WHO USE IT? OR ARE YOU WORRIED THAT IT MIGHT COLLAPSE UNDER ITS OWN WEIGHT, LEAVING ONLY EXPENSIVE PAY-AS-YOU-GO WEBSITES ABLE TO MATCH THE STANDARDS THAT USERS HAVE COME TO EXPECT?

Glossary

audio   To do with sound.

birth certificate   A legal document stating a person's name, date and place of birth.

Cold War   The period from 1945 to 1990, when the United States and the Soviet Union were constantly on the edge of war with each other.

cookies   Small files added to a computer from a website; usually used to make it easier to load the same site again, but sometimes used to check which sites a user visits.

copyright   The law that prevents writers from using others' writing without permission.

download   To transfer information to a computer.

edit   To change the words or appearance of a file or document.

eight-track cartridge   A type of music tape in the 1970s which was bulkier than a cassette and could not record music.

e-mail   Messages sent electronically from one computer to others.

fibre-optic cables   A communication system using glass or plastic threads (rather than traditional metal wires) to send information quickly.

hypertext   An underlined word or phrase that leads the user to another page if the user clicks on it.

idealistic   Believing that the world can become a better place for all who live in it.

interactive (of a type of media)   Allowing a user to react to, and influence something.

invested   Put money in a business to help it grow.

jpeg   A kind of file made up of an image.

media   The name for different types of communication such as the Internet, newspapers, television and radio.

MP3   Sound files that can be sent through the Internet.

organized crime   Large-scale criminal operations run like a business.

profit   Surplus money made when something is sold for more than it cost to make or buy.

resources (in computers)   The different types of files and other information that can run on a computer or be sent from one to another on the Internet.

royalties   Money earned by the creator of something (such as a writer or musician) every time a copy is sold.

satellite   A man-made object sent into outer space.

scam   A dishonest trick, usually designed to steal money from people.

software   Detailed instructions which allow a computer to carry out a job or series of jobs.

Soviet Union   The former name of Russia and some of its neighbouring countries, which was a rival of the United States from 1945 to 1990.

spam   Unwanted e-mails.

video-sharing   Allowing people to add their own videos to a website.

virtual reality   A computer version of the real world, with images and sounds.

Web browser   Software that helps people find their way around the Internet.

Web page   Information such as words, images and sounds consisting of a single computer screen.

website   A collection of Web pages created and managed by a single individual or organization.

World Wide Web   A collection of computer resources, linked together along the Internet.

Further reading

Internet (Straight to the Source) John Hamilton (Abdo 2004)

Connect Online! Student Edition (McGraw Hill 2002)

The Internet (Opposing Viewpoints) James D. Torr (ed) (Greenhaven Press 2005)

The History of the Internet and the World Wide Web Art Wolinsky (Enslow, 2000)

Website links

Coding Horror
www.codinghorror.com/blog/

Make your own website
http://library.thinkquest.org/4658/Website.htm

ConnectSafely
http://www.connectsafely.org/

One Laptop per Child
http://www.laptop.org/

Internet Guide
http://www.internet-guide.co.uk/

SafeKids.com
http://safekids.com/

Index

advertisements 6, 34
applications 27
ARPANET 9, 10, 11, 24

bank statements 32, 33
banking 7, 18, 30, 31, 32
blogs 27, 31
broadband 21

charity 31, 41
computers 8, 9, 10, 12, 13, 14, 20, 21, 23, 24, 25, 28, 33, 36, 38, 40
cookies 35, 44
copyright 17, 44
crime 7, 32, 33, 44

dot-com companies 29, 30
downloads 8, 17, 18, 35, 44

e-mail 7, 8, 10, 11, 25, 30, 37, 40, 44
encyclopedias 22, 23

essays 34, 35

fibre-optic cables 12, 13, 44
films 6, 39

games 27

hypertext 7, 10, 14, 44

identity theft 7, 32, 33
information 7, 9, 10, 12, 14, 16, 21, 22, 23, 31, 33, 34, 36

jobs 35
jpegs 7, 44

magazines 6, 7
media 6, 44
mobile phones 12, 26, 33
MP3 players 16, 17, 44
music 17, 18, 27, 39, 41

networks 9, 11, 13, 24
newspapers 6, 7, 23

passwords 25
personal details 27, 31
plagiarism 35
privacy 35, 43

quizzes 27

radio 23, 38
risks 27, 38, 40
royalties 21, 44

satellite television 12
satellites 9, 45
scams 29, 31, 45
shopping 18
snooping 34, 36, 37
social networking sites 25, 26, 27, 35, 39
software 10, 14, 15, 17, 19, 20, 21, 28, 31, 36, 45
spam 11. 45

telephones 9, 12, 13, 16, 37
television 6, 7, 23, 25, 38

terrorism 37
university 9, 35
Usenet 24, 25

video 26, 27, 41, 45
virtual communities 26
virtual reality 34, 45
viruses 28, 34

Web browser 14, 15, 45
Web pages 7, 45
Web server 14
websites 8, 14, 17, 19, 23, 25, 26, 27, 31, 34, 35, 39, 41, 43, 45